Rafting the Brazos

Rafting the Brazos

Walter McDonald

University of North Texas Press: Denton, Texas

Texas Poets Series General Editor: Richard B. Sale

Library of Congress Cataloging-in-Publication Data

McDonald, Walter.
        Rafting the Brazos.

        I. Title
PS3563.A2914R3   1988   811'.54   88-28073
ISBN 0-929398-00-9

Acknowledgments

I'm deeply grateful to the editors of the following publications in which earlier versions of these poems first appeared, some with different titles:

America: "Moses, at Jordan"
American Poetry Review: "Starting a Pasture"
Ariel (Canada): "The Songs We Fought For"
Artful Dodge: "Night of the Power Outage"
Ascent: "Leaving a Boat on the Brazos"
Blue Unicorn: "Herding the Goats with Collies"
Cape Rock: "Goat Ranching on Hardscrabble"
Chariton Review: "Fishing the Brazos"
　　　　　　　　"The Weatherman Reports the Weather"
Cimarron Review: "Looking Out on the Morning"
College English: "Nights in the San Juan"
Colorado Review: "The Farm at Auction"
Confrontation: "Hit and Run"
Connecticut River Review: "Soaring at Marfa"
Country Journal: "Double Mountain Fork of the Brazos"
Cresset: "Levels"
　　　　　"The Waves at Padre Island"
　　　　　"The Wonder of Dry Fields"
Cross Timbers Review: "Living in Next-Year Country"
CutBank: "Rafting the Brazos"
Descant (Canada): "Following the Dog to Water"
　　　　　　　　　"On the Farm"
Descant (U.S.A.): "Prairie Dogs Live in Lubbock"
Elkhorn Review: "Black Wings Wheeling"
　　　　　　　　"Returning to the Scene"
Fiddlehead (Canada): "Fishing at Fort Hood"
Folio: "On the Den Wall"
Galley Sail Review: "Sandstorms"

Great River Review: "Alone in a Windstorm"
Green Mountains Review: "East of Eden"
                    "In All Low Places"
                    "Reading the Words Again in Winter"
Hampden-Sydney Poetry Review: "Stories We Seem to
                                    Remember"
Images: "First Solo"
              "Sleeping on Cots at Lake Buchanan"
Interim: "Each in its Element"
Kansas Quarterly: "A Brief, Familiar Story of Winter"
Kentucky Poetry Review: "Crop Dusting in a Biplane"
Long Pond Review: "Crosswinds"
                    "The Golden Bowl"
MacGuffin: "Sonnets From the Personals"
Malahat Review (Canada): "Ice Fishing"
                            "The Witness of Dry Plains"
                            "Wonders of the World"
Mississippi Valley Review: "The Common Air"
New Mexico Humanities Review: "Dry Land Farming"
                                "Moving in a Mobile Time"
New Southern Literary Messenger: "Learning the Story of
                                    Scars"
North American Review: "After the Fall of Saigon"
Old Red Kimono: "Taking off in Winter"
Outposts Poetry Quarterly (U.K.): "Hawks, up Close and Far
                                    Away"
Oxford Magazine: "Setting Out Oaks in Winter"
Phoebe: "Open Country"
Pivot: "Alone with a Lantern in Winter"
Poet Lore: "Another Kind of Outdoor Game"
              "Going Away Together"
              "Night of the Scorpion"
Poetry Ireland: "Living on Open Plains"
Poetry Toronto (Canada): "Jacob's Ceiling"

Puerto del Sol: "Out of the Whirlwind"
Re: Artes Liberales: "Grandfather's Farm Near Morton"
Riverwind: "Coming Home"
San Jose Studies: "At Port Aransas"
Scrivener (Canada): "Home"
Seattle Review: "His Side of It"
Silverfish Review: "Drilling on Dry Land"
Sonoma Mandala: "August on Padre Island"
                 "The Picker Takes a Cold Ride to Austin"
South Dakota Review: "High Plains Orchards"
South Florida Poetry Review: "Without Fear of Flying"
Spoon River Quarterly: "Witching"
Sucarnochee Review: "In the Rare Acquisitions Room"
Sunrust: "How the Records Fell"
Sweet Nothings: "At the Stone Café"
Tar River Poetry: "Mainly the Values Change"
Texas Review: "Cicadas"
                 "Driving at Night through Texas"
Waves (Canada): "Grandmother's Last Years"
Weber Studies: "On A Screened Porch in the Country"
West Branch: "Bulls at Sundown"
Widener Review: "Night Shuttle"
Willow Springs: "Dust Devils"
Writers Forum: "The Sting of the Visible"
                 "Trout Fishing in the Rockies"
Zone 3: "In the Attic"

"Nights in the San Juan" was first published by *College English*. Copyright © 1986 by the National Council of Teachers of English. Reprinted by permission. "Rafting the Brazos" and "Starting a Pasture" are reprinted from *Witching on Hardscrabble* (Spoon River Poetry Press). Special thanks to Texas Tech University for faculty development leaves and to the National Endowment for the Arts for a fellowship, which provided the time to write these poems.

CONTENTS

1. HAWKS, UP CLOSE AND FAR AWAY

Starting a Pasture   3
High Plains Orchards   5
After the Fall   6
Hawks, up Close and Far Away   8
The Wonder of Dry Fields   9
Driving at Night through Texas   10
Dry Land Farming   12
Nights in the San Juan   13
Returning to the Scene   14
Trout Fishing in the Rockies   15
The Golden Bowl   16
Bulls at Sundown   17
Taking off in Winter   18
Alone with a Lantern in Winter   20

2. THE STING OF THE VISIBLE

Black Wings Wheeling   23
Fishing the Brazos   24
Stories We Seem to Remember   26
Goat Ranching on Hardscrabble   28
The Sting of the Visible   29
Herding the Goats with Collies   30
Night Shuttle   31
Cicadas   32

Night of the Scorpion   33
Rafting the Brazos   34
Following the Dog to Water   36
First Solo   38
The Songs We Fought For   39

3. IN ALL LOW PLACES

In All Low Places   43
Grandmother's Last Years   44
In the Rare Acquisitions Room   46
Reading the Words Again in Winter   47
On the Den Wall   48
Hit and Run   49
East of Eden   50
Sonnets From the Personals   52
The Common Air   53
Moses, at Jordan   55
Another Kind of Outdoor Game   56
A Brief, Familiar Story of Winter   59
The Weatherman Reports the Weather   60
The Picker Takes a Cold Ride to Austin   62
His Side of It   63
Moving in a Mobile Time   64
Night of the Power Outage   66
At the Stone Café   67
Sleeping on Cots at Lake Buchanan   68
Leaving a Boat on the Brazos   69
Coming Home   70

4. OUT OF THE WHIRLWIND

      Grandfather's Farm Near Morton 75
      Witching 76
      On the Farm 77
      The Witness of Dry Plains 78
      Living on Open Plains 79
      Open Country 80
      Sandstorms 81
      Crosswinds 82
      Out of the Whirlwind 84
      Drilling on Dry Land 85
      Levels 86
      Soaring at Marfa 87
      Prairie Dogs Live in Lubbock 88
      Dust Devils 89
      Living in Next-Year Country 90
      The Farm at Auction 91

5. WITHOUT FEAR OF FLYING

      Crop Dusting in a Biplane 95
      Looking Out on the Morning 96
      Learning the Story of Scars 98
      Going Away Together 99
      Each in its Element 101
      Double Mountain Fork of the Brazos 102
      Home 103

On A Screened Porch in the Country   104
August on Padre Island   105
Mainly the Values Change   106
The Waves at Padre Island   107
At Port Aransas   108
Alone in a Windstorm   109
Fishing at Fort Hood   110
Without Fear of Flying   112
Ice Fishing   113
How the Records Fell   115
Wonders of the World   116
In the Attic   117
Jacob's Ceiling   119
Setting Out Oaks in Winter   120

HAWKS, UP CLOSE AND FAR AWAY

Starting a Pasture

This far out in the country no one is talking,
no rescue squads row by in boats to prairie land
so dry the Ogallala water table drops
three feet every year. The digger rams down
through dirt no plow has turned. In the heat
I let my mind run wild. For days I've thought
the world is ending, the red oaks turning red
again, the last geese there could be
stampeding from the north, surviving
to show us the only hope, the tips of their
arrow formations pointing the way. So many birds,
if the world doesn't end, this will be for Canada
the year of the locust. I shake my head
at my schemes, and sweat flies: cattle
on cottonland. The market for beef
is weak, the need for cotton constant.

I might as well raise goats and sheep as cows,
or trap for bounty the wolves and coyotes
that claim my fields at night. I might as well
rent a steam shovel and dig a lake deep as an ark,
empty my last irrigation well to fill it
green enough for geese on the flyway
both seasons. I could raise trout and channel cat,
horses and bees, gazelles and impala imported
from other deserts, two of each kind
of animals in a dying world.

Sun going down,
the last hole dug, the last post dropped
and tamped tight enough to hold three strands of wire,
I toss the digger in the pickup between bales
of barbed wire ready for stringing, the calves
I bought last week already overdue, the feedbill
mounting. My father used to say a man could lift
a bull if he'd practice on a calf each day.
Pulling my gloves back on, I lift the first bale
out and nail the end, uncoil the wire and nail it
tight to the posts. And while it turns dark
I go on stretching and nailing until I don't care
how many neighbors drive by with their lights on,
honking, sticking their heads out the windows
    and laughing.

4

High Plains Orchards

These twigs may be an orchard yet.
Grow peaches on the plains most years
and reap heat-blighted leaves, bindweed
and Bermuda grass the certain crops.
All prairie dirt is blow-sand
trampled by hooves, herds on the prowl
thousands of years for water scarce as trees.

My great-greats came here trying to choke back
bull-necked oxen, backs bowed west
and gorging prairie grass like pastures of heaven.
Here they stopped, refused to budge, or died.
On land so flat no wonder people pray. Bad luck
explodes next door, tornadoes that swirl down
out of clouds black as Bibles. With no mountains
to hide behind, homes are glass and love goes on.
Trees are our only valleys.

My neighbor's horses picket my gate
for their daily pears. For luck, I promise apples.
Each winter, I jab down arrows of new trees,
mound up the dirt and wait for buds
here in a zone so rough no trees grow native.
Last March, someone with a buzz saw
killed all pecans in my neighbor's orchard.
Lord. No one need offer an excuse for trees.

After the Fall

Hunting, a man keeps his rifle steady,
safety ready to flick off and fire.
You don't get many shots out here.
Long tubes of cactus, the flat flesh
of prickly pears, loose rocks that trip you up

every step of the way. None but a fool
would hunt like this except for meat. Crouched,
I try to piece together why I'm here,
nothing about this flat, dry land like Vietnam
but my sun-burned eyes and ears. My trailer house

squats on this desert like an old woman
taking a rock from her shoe. I saw my kids
invent a game after the school bus dropped them
by the side of the road and roared off
back to town, the first time I had seen them

in a week. He loves me, they said in turn, he
loves me not, snapping off thorns like pulling needles.
When I was a boy, my logger father moved us near
    a forest,
the thickest woods I ever saw, the new pines trunk
    to trunk
for miles, stunted, their stubby branches snagged,

shoving for room. His crew slashed through trees
for weeks and never left our sight. He said
the virgin woods where he grew up were like

6

a circus tent, the trees massive, scattered,
only their top branches touching, a green roof

shutting off the light so no shrubs grew,
the forest like the stillness before dawn.
He said a boy could ride a horse for hours
at full gallop and easily avoid the trees,
or silently stalk bear or game downwind,

the layers of leaves soft as fur, the forest
like an aviary, the branches bright with song.
He never found the time to take me hunting.
My only rides were moves to other woods.
He cut the trees because he had to live,

like me. But I forgave him years ago.
The pine that broke back into him, high branches
caught in a noose of limbs and swaying,
cracked all his ribs like match sticks. I never
saw him again, except chin up, in the coffin.

Climbing over these loose stones, I keep
a tight balance between thorns, counting
the years since Vietnam, like my daughters
squeezing a desert cactus in their hands,
their eyes pulling the sharp facts like petals.

Hawks, up Close and Far Away

Steady as clocks, three hawks keep circling
overhead. It could be mice at a trough,
a pair of rabbits far from a burrow.
No buzzards, which often group and glide
in a black spiraling mobile,

but hawks, which always are alone,
until today. As long as I'm here whittling
in a deer-hide chair under the only oak,
they'll circle over whatever's near me on earth.
I could get up and go inside for water

and soon it would all be over. Hawks have always
been my friends, but one at a time, up high,
keeping dry skies at ease, the way I work
each week, checking tight barbed-wire fences,
time enough for scruples back in the kitchen,

watching my wife cook venison. Mesquite stick
finally whittled like a flute, I push up and start inside,
pulling the Stetson low against the sun,
mounting up step by step a porch that squeaks
too loud to hear wings diving at my back.

The Wonder of Dry Fields

Because coyotes are lean, we own them,
beggars that prowl parched fields at midnight.
At noon, if we stand too long in one place,
our boot soles burn. Only twice in my life
such a drought, the last one years ago,

before Saigon. Our crop that year was buzzards,
like watermelon vines black after a frost. Now,
Saigon blooms often in my dreams, rockets,
monsoons too deep to wade, except awake.
I stare at skies too peaceful to believe.

A man riding alone carries his rifle for rattlers.
Our chidren sleep with only me to protect them,
nothing I haven't saved them from for years. Coyotes
fearing all evil on horseback come out at night,
feeding on fawns. With little feed for cattle and goats,

we dump all bales we can in distant pastures.
And still they starve, deer stumbling
down deep arroyos a hundred yards from the barn.
Wherever deer go, coyotes are sure to follow,
tuck their tails and slink to the dump

where we save skinned bones for burning.
Mending the barbed-wire fences, we wonder
how many days until thunder, how many
steers we should auction, how many
coyotes fear guns if they're starving.

DRIVING AT NIGHT THROUGH TEXAS

Tonight we race the quarter moon,
counting the miles by pelts on a highway
black as a Bible and seldom used.
Truckers don't even blink their brights,
our low beams shining no more
than fifty feet ahead, nothing to see

but blips of silver dividing the road,
and cactus flashing by on either side.
In our lights, even thin mesquites
flip by faster than us
the wrong way, miles of the same
straight road rolling beneath us

like a player piano cranking the same old
country and western tune that takes us
home. I'd like to hit the switch
and drive in moonlight, but you believe
in deer and cattle-crossing signs,
although we haven't seen a thing

on roads we couldn't thump
and keep on going, wondering for miles
what madness drove it to our lights
and what it was, armadillo or rabbit,
certainly not skunk, nothing through open
windows flinging your hair this wild

10

but sweet vinegar-sage and cactus,
no stubborn bulls or mule deer
straddling our lane, nothing above us
but stars and a quarter moon moving
slowly and farther off no matter
how fast, how many miles we go.

DRY LAND FARMING

All summer we ditched for runoff
from rain that never came
to save our storm-proof cotton,
hot sun squeezing the bolls

like sponges. The only clouds
were in our minds, the sky
day after day dry as the Astrodome.
We prayed for all the storms of August

to drown our hybrid stalks, test us
with forty days of thunderclouds
and save our wretched fibers.
Nothing, not prayer, not silver iodide

could bring a drop, and all of us
were sailors, curses that rained
all during harvest, and snow
that purified the fields all winter.

NIGHTS IN THE SAN JUAN

Bed and chairs, table and stove,
home for a week in the mountains.
Because the logs are stacked

we love them, two rooms
that would be a shanty
on the plains. Cold water faucet

that drips all night.
Bare ceiling, two beams split.
A board floor easy to sweep clean

through the cracks.
Curtains too short, too thin
to block out the moon.

Nothing is level, flush.
You sleep against me
on the uphill side,

the wood fire cold by midnight.
The forest so still, so dark
I can hear stars burning.

Returning to the Scene

We weave up San Juan trails
through spruce and piñon,
heeding the fear of snakes
with sticks, like stoking a fire.

Mosquitoes slow and wavering
hover like mobiles in Eden,
hazy green, grown-over, the way
we left it. Light drips from moss

swamp-like on every bough.
Some snow remains, trickles
in streams we leap across.
We've read about fires and floods,

climbers in shirt sleeves freezing
in blizzards. We carry sticks
in our hands like spears, though nothing
here seems wild. We believe

where we are heading has no name,
no picnic tables and no trails,
and we will know it when we arrive
panting, slapping mosquitoes.

Trout Fishing in the Rockies

Near Creede where the Rio Grande runs clear
we backpack creels downstream, a flick,
flick to get the tight line flexing.

At first the pools back of boulders
for practice, sometimes a perfect cast
and strike as if winter never happened.

Crouched, we point at this pool,
that cutbank under the moss,
pretending trout can't see us.

Knowing trout are corrupt with hunger,
we offer flies like bribes.
Flicking our wrists out over stones

we reel in cutthroats and browns
from swift water as if nothing
but trout could save us.

THE GOLDEN BOWL

Days this fast should happen only
at puberty and death. Drowning in bills
and children, in bed too often with a disease
called dread, we race the clock to work
and back, boiling in a greenhouse on wheels,
parallel with others growing madder

by the mile. Only a turnoff
with our street's tin name keeps us
from following a pace car racing west
out of this desert town we've lived in
for years, away from petty thefts
of minutes we risk to explore our lives—

brief encounters doing dishes,
a midnight waltz across the bedroom
before falling again for that old ruse
that promises sweet dreams, sometimes
an alley rendezvous holding hands
offering trash to the dumpster,

the answer to all loss. Alone
in moonlight, we toss it all inside
and lock the gate to keep the old dogs safe.
Hands locked and swinging like the tree rope
dangling frayed, we enter the house,
the shining house, and close the door.

16

Bulls at Sundown

Like a foreign god, the old herd bull
hauls himself uphill, rump and horns
see-sawing side to side. He's all alone
this close to darkness, bells of all cows

muffled by the barn, sweet odor
of fresh milk lazy from the stalls.
Calves waul and canter to the troughs,
shoving each other off and stumbling,

all of this having all and nothing to do
with him. Always in his corral of steel bars
a trough of grain is set, and so he comes
slowly between a ball of orange fire

in the west and dark rain-clouds,
time enough for standing still
and eating, swishing his tail
at horse flies always out of reach,

sun going down, an ache in his bones
like winter winds too soon,
the chaff tasteless and thin
like dry snow sticking to his lips.

Taking Off in Winter

I taxi out between two banks of snow,
the airport opened again, my headset
crackling clearance for this jet to land,
for Cessna two-niner delta
to climb and maintain five thousand.

I jockey the throttle behind planes
taxiing one by one
the way we used to ride round-ups
down canyons, searching for strays.
All summer we bowed our legs

around the barrels of stallions,
our hard bunks better than the prairie
we slept on half the time. If dirt
was soft, we scooped out hip-holes
and mounded sand for pillows.

All winter we rode to church on Sundays,
the foreman giving Mondays
to all who claimed to worship.
Female voices filled us with incense,
our throats clogged with dust

from a thousand hooves, our chapped lips
splitting to reach the high notes,
red hymnals of the Sacred Harp
swaying in our fists, our bowed legs
catching the fire of the spirit,

18

the whole church of boots stomping
with new wine of the Sabbath,
like now, moving fast down a runway
and rising, lips healed,
scorched eyes able to see.

ALONE WITH A LANTERN IN WINTER

Smoke climbs hot lantern beams. The dog
barks sharply for attention. I reach
to find him lifting the dish of his skull
for all the fingers I can give.

Here in the dark, I hear a peacock
screaming, his shrill gargle begging praise
all through the night. In weeks,
he'll parade and preen himself,

the ground thawing, he'll believe,
because of him, his peafowls hatching
the finest flock in the world, the earth
abundant with food under his feet.

We'll sit out here with the dog,
without the need of fire, counting
the hours we've spent like this.
Those nights have power to raise dead trees

to life, turn stones to moss, move the sun
out of its orbit north again. We'll think
of bodies on All Souls' Night that mingle,
the bones dug up that shine.

THE STING OF THE VISIBLE

Black Wings Wheeling

A man riding on hardscrabble
carries his rifle loaded,
ready to throw down on rattlers

or wolves attacking calves
in dry arroyos. Out here,
killing's always in season.

Barbed wire alone can't turn stray
cattle back, if they smell water.
Skies are blue and vacant,

the earth is white caliche.
The way to pray in the saddle
is to ride slumped over,

spine bent like a question,
trusting horse sense and grace
to arrive wherever you're going

on a range never green enough
under hawks spiraling,
keeping a delicate balance.

FISHING THE BRAZOS

Fishing in hardscrabble, a man keeps his tackle
handy, ready to rise up and walk on water.
Rattlesnakes there are bad,
sneaking up behind and shaking like gourds
of holy rollers in tent meetings, half the congregation
speaking in tongues and quaking, some picking up
    snakes
and writhing, on fire in the spirit, ignoring
us boys outside and laughing.

Years later, the rod in your fingertips
waiting for ghost fingers lighter than nibbles
on the line, you may wake to moccasins
gliding like ghosts on the water, rising
to claim the rocks as theirs. Better to give up
and live to fish in a shallow pool than fight
the old serpent on his ground—such a thrashing
and wicked dying no fish would rise to any bait
for hours.

Go where the rocks are dry,
where frogs sprawl openly on stumps, birds
fight in the hot air for the begging grounds,
and there cast out your lures for bass,
using the surface bugs to bring them up
among the weeds and cattails. Even with a stringer
full of fish you will still have to reach down
into the waters with respect for what lies hidden,
still have to pick your way through dangling twigs
of mesquite trees, over stones and caliche holes
back to the car you've waded from up to your knees
in cactus, over your head in thorns.

Stories We Seem to Remember

My father fished the Ouachita swamps
in winter, a sheet of ice so thin
even cast bait broke it,
squirrels sleeping overhead,
thousands of ducks at rest
after the Canadian flyway.

He was ten, able to go anywhere
alone, having no mother,
a father who turned corn liquor
out by the barrel, gone half the time
running his corn to market.

My father cooked his own stringer of fish,
slept by the warmth of the still
hidden by cypress, his arms
covered with chiggers and mosquito bites,
his boots the boots of his father
stuffed with bags of fish scales.
The first moccasin struck only a boot,
a fish-boy his uncles called Boots.

The next one gashed his heel
when he swam naked with my mother
the year of my birth,
the night the river bled
from my father's knife slash
in a swamp he'd gone back to visit,
no place I've seen but seem to remember,
and a tail lashing through water,
thrashing a current of blood.

GOAT RANCHING ON HARDSCRABBLE

I believed the world was thicket,
our farm like all farms—nothing but pastures
fenced tight against rattlers and bear grass
only goats could eat.

My father cursed each goat he foraged,
grudging the time it took to sell them,
fighting mesquite all winter—all those fires,
snapped sawblades, tractors overheated
trying to drag mesquite fields level.

Mornings, we stacked cactus and trunks
and roots stripped white as bones,
and doused thorn piles with coal oil.
Goats foraged all day down the fence,
our tractor and buzz saw growling
under billowing smoke, the whole world burning.

The Sting of the Visible

My father fenced our goats
with chicken wire, jerking bulky bales
from post to post to keep goats home,
a web of thick mesh they could see.

They believed, all but a few
that hooked their nubbin horns
under tight fence and gagged.
When I was ten he strung the first

electric wire in the county,
a single strand stretched to the edge
of wonder. Green tassels tempted the billies.
Without the seen chicken wire, goats lusted

for oats in forbidden fields. They pranced,
the filament zipped, zipped, goats
baaed like sheep, whirled back to the wire
like a magnet, crying and pinging away.

One night, I cut the current off
and let the goats run wild,
then cried and danced at dawn
to the ping of my father's belt.

HERDING THE GOATS WITH COLLIES

Goats ran, stumbling on shale
and leaping up steep arroyos.
Dogs turned tame goats into cowards.
Goats were the ghosts of their world,

spooked by their shadows. Stampeded,
they bounced like antelopes, zig-zagged
and stabbed themselves with their horns.
The dogs were trained to herd

fat cattle too lazy to run.
Cows went wherever they were told
in slow motion, chewing their cud
and trudging, full udders swaying.

Dogs worried the clopping hooves
by barking, nipping and dodging.
Scared goats bolted away
at first bark. Dogs chased,

impressed with their voices,
barking full speed and nipping,
the bobbing goats spraying a trail
of pellets all the way home.

NIGHT SHUTTLE

We'd leave after dark, windows down
to catch the first cool breeze all day.
Three to a seat, we squeezed
for elbow room, for pillows
and canteens and bags of snacks.

Before Daddy could shift the Ford
to high, Grandma raised her snuff can
to her lips, spittooing the brown
sweet stink. Hands on his knees,
leg and wide elbow gouging me,

Grandpa told us again how wagons
bounced when he was a boy,
no deep-pile cushions to sit on,
no sirree. Restless, without light
to read our stack of comics by,

my sister and I sneaked punches
at each other behind Grandpa's neck,
even though we knew the first
who hit him would get spanked.
For years we shuttled to Arkansas

by night in that black car
to bury Ozark relatives I never knew,
grandparents falling asleep,
our mother silent by the window,
staring at dark plains speeding past.

Cicadas

Summer nights we ran for miles
around and around the only willow
in town, the long sheaves lashing our
vision dizzy, like crepe paper doorways
on Halloween, cicadas suddenly
clattering down on us, bursting
from thousands of willow limbs
like bats, like blind bats bumping
the leaves, banging their horn heads
against our faces, cicadas screaming
like klaxons, all of us screaming
and running faster
and faster from death.

All summer we entered the dark
limbs of that willow like a haunted
house filled with ghosts.
By winter, on branches like reeds,
we found them exposed, only
blunt shells split down the back.
We read them in silence as tokens,
as evidence of things not seen,
the thin shells clinging,
riding the whip of the wind
like sheets left behind by ghosts,
like hope gone underground
that would rise someday in new bodies
and haunt us the rest of our lives.

NIGHT OF THE SCORPION

Night of the scorpion, night of ice packs
and ankle swelling, my father tumbling stones
of a chimney fallen to rubble years ago,
fierce to kill whatever stung me.

In fever I rolled and tossed, saw his shadow
high in the willows, cast by the car lights,
broad back and head like a stinger
lunging from side to side, stones crashing
like thunder, like ninepins in the mountains.

All night I crawled through fire and forest,
gnashing my teeth, slicing my knees
on brimstones hissing and scuttling away.
Steam rising from fissures screened demons
writhing and reaching for me. All night,
spiders died, mice died in their nests,
rocks burst and scattered like wind.

All day the next day my father slept,
unable to save me, his fingers raw
to the bone, my whole foot cold, swollen,
but a foot I could stand on
down on the same rubbled earth.

Rafting the Brazos

All summer after chores,
we dragged our tractor inner tubes,
patched like Uncle Murphy's face on Sunday,
and launched them on the wide flat water.

We shoved them out to the middle,
kicking our feet like frogmen. Splashing,
our dogs barking on the bank behind us,
we cursed each other for distance.

Someone always cheated. At fourteen
games are serious as sex. Everything
has rules and everybody breaks them.
And so the day Durwood Stanley slumped over

on his tube and dropped his paddle
we passed him and jeered at whatever stunt
he was pulling, watching nothing but brown
water turn foam-white up ahead.

Each of us fought for flumes
through the boulders, the only way
to keep on breathing, catching our breath
and plunging under water, each man for himself,

boiling in hell and out again, back on the Brazos
mud-brown, flowing as if it hadn't happened.
Laughing, wiping our eyes and bragging our ride
was the damnedest ever, we finally saw

Durwood's empty red and blue patched tube bob by,
riding high on the river, bulging like lungs
held too long, about to burst.
Later, our fathers reasoned the doctor found

no water in his lungs, nothing we could do
to save him, no matter how long we pumped
after we pulled him out, how long
we huffed and blew into his rubber mouth.

FOLLOWING THE DOG TO WATER

Where the trail drops off
and diamondbacks lay claim
to anything that aches for water,
we enter the canyon with lanterns
and guns, get a grip on the dogs
and pair off in moonlight
tracking both sides of the creek.

What we are after knows he must run
but not why, the world gone mad
around him, everything he meets
hissing and backing away, or running
for him and firing. He believes
water can save him.
He has come wading this creek

down with raccoons and rabbits
he has hunted for years.
He will kill anything in his way
for water, like the child
that ran to him at sundown
with a leash, arms flung out
and hoarse with calling.

He believes behind all boulders
are rattlers,
dogs with dry mouths,
lanterns he cannot lose.
He wades up to his chest
in water that recedes
whenever he laps it.

He would give himself up
to sleep and glide home
on his belly, but he hears
high, hysterical barking,
gunshots around him,
rocks chipping
and whining of water.

First Solo

Giddy, I swayed in a Cessna
rising, no limit to the lift
the light wings found bouncing
through thermals. Sunlight
spun from the blades in a blur
I could see through. Lurching
alone in the yonder, I looped
the hollow clouds, the wild blue.

The Songs We Fought For

Heart-breakers sang at Rusty's, the last bar
north of Slaton. *Stand by yo'r man,*
they sobbed to the swing of crystal earrings,
or scowled and doubled up ring-knuckled fists

and growled, *Ain't gonna be yo'r honky-tonk woman
anymore.* Their innocent, wicked faces
were safe behind the same thick makeup,
their nests of sprayed hair floated yellow-blue

in spotlights and smoke of local men and women
groping for their lives. It's gone, torn down
like the drive-in, two midnight places
people went to get away from lives more boring

than the plains. One young singer from Austin
flirted with us like a school girl, sitting
on every lap. Some yelled and tossed their hats,
as if they'd stayed on a bull for eight seconds.

Up close, her eyes flared wide, as if whispering
save me. Billy Ray crushed a beer can in his fist,
and foam shot out and splattered on the floor.
Billy Ray stared at deer heads on the wall.

We knew she couldn't last, trying too hard
to be human. Those hard-voiced untouchable women
gave us the tunes we wanted, the same old wailing
on stage that made fist-fights and a dance

enough to dream about all week in the saddle,
roping another bawling calf to castrate and burn
with a branding iron, touching our own bruised ribs
and teeth, wincing and spitting blood.

IN ALL LOW PLACES

In All Low Places

In Florida, men upside down in circus tents
swing back and forth to applause
and waltzes, legs locked,
hands chalked to catch their partners.

In Carlsbad Caverns, bats grasp
stone ceilings and swing like bells,
millions of mosquitoes dying
in bellies before our eyes.

Outside Durango, a man dismounts in snow
by the barbed wire, wades mountain pastures
not ready for his herd, the bulls
about to kick the barn down.

In Wales, men up from mile-deep mines
lift their eyes to the dawn,
their smudged skin dark as their vests,
their eyes and lips bone-white.

In Kashmir, widows in muslin robes
lift their hands to the mountains
and pray for hours. Their bracelets
glitter, their dark arms tremble.

GRANDMOTHER'S LAST YEARS

Whatever she lifted hardened,
water in a winter bucket,
potato tubers in July,
her ankles stiffer up the steps

each month. How she kept raising
berries and pears for neighbors
was the puzzle, all that
hobbling over and back,

bearing bushels a day all summer.
Boards of her porch curled up
like bean pods dried in the compost.
Limping step by step, she straddled

planks like cross ties to her door,
and rested, the high ceiling fan floating
flute flute above her rocker.
Breathing too fast, creased lips

moist as the snuff her granny
used to dip, she rocked hard, hard,
trying to catch up with her heart.
She must have thought

of all to be done before dark,
cherry tomatoes turning soft,
okra stiffening on the stalks,
peaches to pick before beetles

stripped the sweet nubbed pits.
For she took a hard grip
on the rocker arms
and lifted herself all the way up,

stopped at the well
and drank from her own dipper,
hearing high in the dark pecan
a new cawing.

In The Rare Acquisitions Room

Glossy, the faces of the Holy Family
perfect in smooth detail,
this fourteenth-century oil-on-board
was hung in this mansion
surrounded by bluebonnets
before I was born. The artist lived

before Chaucer's birth. The baby
in a cradle stained like Texas mesquite
stares up, dark eyebrows bushy.
Leaning, I see that the artist
posed a man, maybe himself,
his daring claim on immortality.

The face of Mary is so real
if I could reach through the glass
I could shake the artist's
small medieval hand, meticulous,
the brow of Joseph behind her
knotted over this puzzle

of birth, his vestments
more like a Venice merchant's
than a carpenter's,
the details of his frown
preserved forever like a bone.

READING THE WORDS AGAIN IN WINTER

The bones in the silence are down there,
we believe, but who would dig them up?
The dirt is level at last. Lazy men

who never mowed, who sprawled in trucks and smoked
and never patched the sinking plots
have all been fired. Now, hosts of grave men

faithful to their tasks patrol in city trucks
bristling with spades and steel rakes,
and crowbars to pry bowed headstones straight.

And here they stand, the facts chiseled
in marble, both stones side by side,
as we left them. I could leap through my eyes

down under dirt into those caskets.
But hesitate, as I did as a child, my hand
on the cold doorknob of my parents' room,

at midnight, too old to confess
I heard scratching sounds outside
too close to ignore.

On the Den Wall

This was a trophy shot, a mile-long kill
through steel and cross hairs on the heart,
this telescope sight a short cut to a cliff
it took hours to climb to uphill,
crossing arroyos through juniper and spruce.
There they rested, whiter, more graceful

than big-horn sheep in zoos, fearing no evil
they could not smell. The ram stood alone
on a stone, horns curled, sweeping his eyes
over a million trees where something below him
flashed faster than his heart could beat
and leap away.

HIT AND RUN

She is loosening my tie
with the slowest hands, fingers
that fan out through my hair.
I try opening my eyes,
but thumbs warm as lips
glide over them.
The siren coming through snow
is for me alone.
My knuckles are bleeding,
freezing to bricks.
The ambulance arrives softly,
blue light beaming, beaming.
This lady leans down as if
listening for my heart,
her breasts familiar as sleep.
I lie still in her arms
this enchanted evening in snow
I feel myself becoming.
When they lead her away
I try to hold on,
but they are lifting
my feet and shoulders
to a bed too narrow
for anyone but me.

East of Eden

Eve fed the snake for years,
  down on his belly, flicked
    from the garden by an angel's foot.

Alone for the first and only time
  in his life, head weaving,
    he lapped the dust of their wandering.

Down in the briars he chaffed
  and often bled, nicking himself
    on stones he learned to curve

and undulate across. He followed
  wherever they went, huddled
    in thunder, hearing the death-

screams of lambs, the roaring
  of unnamed beasts. His tongue
    taught them caution, the wisdom

of testing the wind. The tines
  of his tongue hissed ideas—
    in drought, how to find blood,

how to live in the sand without God,
without myths of living water,
how to hone sharp points

of spears. They watched him crawl
softly and low, before striking.
He taught every trick of his heart,

coiled, like family, swearing
two was the perfect number.
He told them to strike

two perfect flints together.
By firelight they studied his eyes,
his ivory fangs.

SONNETS FROM THE PERSONALS

We read the want ads to each other,
shaking our heads at how many ways
to call it: bloodflow, the simple
touching. Discreet, unrushed,

inexpensive. Sweet modeling,
the Texas Dozen (fifteen
rosy, long-stemmed). Cover girls,
singing strip-o-grams. Lace Princess

Pleasure Palace. Let us help
make someone happy. Strictly true

legitimate massages. Seven years'
dependability, Sissie, Gypsie,

and Leigh. Nude modeling. Tammy
the radiator doctor. Complete body works.

The Common Air

Rust begs for air—
fire begs, vacuums, gills
straining for oxygen
under tons of ocean,

and medics pounding the chest
of that man collapsed by a billboard.
They puff his rubber lips
like a balloon: the face fills
and sags, fills and caves-in
like his chest, aching to breathe
on its own.

The aircrew in this theatre
tosses all they own
overboard to stay aloft,
their pilot nurses the controls
for fifty more feet of air
to lift them above the white cliffs
of Dover, the shot-up bomber
banging, hanging by the skin of its wings.
Young men bailing out show us
how to face death by water.

That man in baggy khaki
slumped on the fender of a car
watches the medics, sucks in his
tongue with each deep breath
and rolls it out, gasping.

At last, they collapse their kit
and all of us catch the drift
of the wind. They lift a bed
full of body through doors
and rage off down the street,
blue lights flashing,

flashing. The night
is full of air we use
and give back to each other,
deep breaths we take, stepping
down off the curb, going our ways
as if nothing's happened.

Moses, At Jordan

As close as he can ever go,
the cliff hot through his sandals,
rocks scattered like bones

of those who died in the desert.
His hips burn, he wants to rest,
but he will never see this far again.

These olive groves are theirs
for the taking, thatched roofs steaming
in the first rain he has smelled

in years. Between him and the orchards
is a stone-path steady as faith.
Ridge upon ridge of hills roll on

forever, layered with clouds like wool.
He knows if he had entered this valley
spread before him like a table,

this promised land flowing with rivers,
he could at last have lain down
under a roof of olives all his own.

ANOTHER KIND OF OUTDOOR GAME

> *My apple trees will never get across*
> *and eat the cones under his pines.*   —Frost

I'm stripping my neighbor's grapes
from the pear tree. Over the gray
picket fence, vines that slithered
through pear leaves years ago
have taken root. Fat as a python

they cling when I shake them, hissing
high in the tree, leaves so tight
I can't see what's above.
We meet at the fence like a border.
What were we doing all these years?

Tending gardens, our children's bones
broken and growing like vines.
He never climbs my tree for grapes,
three sides of his fence a vineyard.
He says we could sever the vines,

release the pears branch by branch.
But mounting a tree not made for climbing
I try unwinding the clock
to give these serpent vines a chance.
We've carried a twelve-foot ladder

from his garage, wedged it through limbs
squeezed like a wheat shock.
Step by step, squinting,
I shoulder up through branches
and pears dangling like bells.

On the top rung in darkness,
buried in vines like kudzu,
I grab one thick as my thumb
and haul it hand over hand
as if climbing—pears, leaves,

clusters of green grapes stripping
and hissing. I hurl the whole mass
outward, coils suddenly
dropping in my face, dangling
hundreds of grapes like snake eggs.

I tell myself pears, fences.
Below stipples of shade
I see tips of fence like lances.
His vines are crushing my pears,
but what's the fuss?

I plant one foot on the neck
of a branch, lean out and grab a vine
and thrash it down, killing
pears and grapes I can't save,
pruning for next year and the next.

We haul them down like battle flags
the way we cover holes our dogs dig
over the years, to keep from quarreling.
It takes a fence here in the city
to live. His dogs are old,

and mine's a Doberman.
Most things, we know,
don't like a fence, and sometimes
we don't either. It takes work
to keep on being neighbors.

A Brief, Familiar Story of Winter

Trees are telling the story of harvest.
The wind is listening, murmuring oh
and dying. Leaves have only one month more

to listen. They glitter in the sun,
flutter like friends in a parlor
fanning themselves and flushing.

The bark has heard it all before,
thick-skinned like a snake
that cannot shed. The taproots

hear in whispers, swelling
each time they hear the old, old story.
They shove into grains of sand

and take all they can give to heartwood.
Chilled zylem lifts the last fluid
upward from the tips of roots

like salmon leaping the rapids,
all branches waiting like bears,
leaves on all limbs trembling.

THE WEATHERMAN REPORTS THE WEATHER

Last night I showed the jet stream crash near the coast
of Canada, pull out over the tip of Texas
and leave the States high over Maine.
I drew a drastic U, a manic-depressive weather
spawning squall lines, the highs and lows
of regions under siege.

The jet stream diving did not show boys
taking a pickup joy-riding during my report,
spinning down a ditch where it flipped and rolled.
The boys fourteen and twelve will not grow old
and bored enough to watch my storm warnings,
barometer falling, the fickle jet stream

diving while policemen climb slow steps
and ring doorbells of boys downtown
on slabs cold as the predicted low.
My map won't show the crosses on that road,
or four last week in Garza County, or thousands
where the jet stream passed last year.

I'd have to draw so small they'd overlap
like tracks, cross-hatched like the stock exchange.
I can't report such things as finance
and behavior. Weather's a science:
it makes nothing happen. Tornadoes
and slick roads won't harm someone

not in a hurry or in the way, and floods
are floods because we live too close.
I let the news and brokers talk of death by drowning,
crashes, leaps from their bankers' ledges.
It's all I can do to understand
the dew point during drought, why winds die

and where they go, forecasts I knew were perfect
that shift under my feet like sand,
the wide, true shots from satellites deep in space.
I give it straight, no news, no predictions
on Super Bowls or children's fate,
not anyone's children, not yours, not mine.

The Picker Takes a Cold Ride to Austin

In snow, all rattlesnakes in Texas
hibernate. Queasy on a borrowed Harley,
strung out on greasy chicken
and french fries from Abilene,
I lean into fat flakes
stinging like the widow's kisses

after last night's gig in Lubbock.
If I'd gone with Jim Bob and the band
I'd be in Austin, still have a job
and money. Dark, and snow fast
in the hill country, ninety,
a hundred miles to go

and I can't see the road.
Snow sticks to my lashes,
I'm wiping them dry
and squinting. Nothing
but ditches keeps me steady,
the road so white I'm blind.

Might as well pull over,
coil up with a den of rattlers,
but I feel a new song coming
and keep on straddling asphalt,
chasing sad words like snow
swirling into my headlight.

His Side of It

And on the way anywhere she'd get out,
climb down another canyon, risking her neck
along the edge. Revving the engine
I'd crush another can and dump it,
always the same flat clatter downhill.

Finally she'd stagger back,
arms filled with lava,
petrified stumps, anything hard.
By then I'd be waiting with the trunk lid up,
beer sorry and horny,

shoving aside antlers
and gnarled roots for space.
And off we'd go down the canyon
for fossils or shells, arrowheads,
whatever she couldn't get enough of alone.

How many times that dry summer
did canyons save what we had?
All summer she led me
loaded with stones uphill and cursing,
but after we stacked her relics like a grave,

before the long climb out
we'd meet on a bed of flint chips,
ignoring snakes and indifferent trucks
somewhere beyond a blur of thistles,
her skin hammered with sand like gold leaf.

Moving in a Mobile Time

For weeks we warned we were leaving.
They sent melons and cakes
each day for brunch, hung gold
and spangled balls in their gardens,

hired bands that played good jazz
past midnight, parties
that started each day by five
in the cool shade of magnolias.

Neighbors leaned low and whispered
or bent back handsome heads
and laughed, hands balancing canapes
and champagne. We tried saying

how much each couple meant, how much
we'd miss them. We danced each dance alone
like lovers. We heard jets
departing in darkness over the trees,

no other sounds but jazz and laughter,
their gardens like lighted islands.
Even the night the truck pulled out
with all we owned, and we were late,

no one noticed the *sold* sign,
our packed car in the driveway,
our traveling clothes. We shook hands
with couples not deep in talk, and danced

one dance with strangers. We whispered
we were leaving, and people we didn't know
embraced and kissed us.
Some waved goodbye-smoke like signals

and the band kept playing jazz.
We left by the locked side gate
and crossed the street to a car
with license tags already foreign.

NIGHT OF THE POWER OUTAGE

We swim slow laps, four strokes
from lip to lip, our apartment pool
in summer. Rising halfway across,
we kiss in five black feet of water.

No moon, no lights on anywhere.
The stars stand still. Shoved
by waves of our own slow motion,
we sway weightless on our toes,

touching each other. Candles may hiss
and flicker out. If city lights stay off
for hours, let them. All night
under stars we could move like this.

AT THE STONE CAFÉ

The waitress leans across with ketchup
for our chicken-fried steaks and beans.
Rouged, perfumed, she exposes a flared
white cleavage. She is some local boy's
Sweet Darlin'. She waltzes off,

humming some country and western tune
that makes her human. Sunlight slices
between her thighs. At the counter,
she cuts a pie for two cowboys she knows.
One rises and whispers in her ear. She winks

and flips his hat, leans back and sips her coffee.
They turn and study whoever enters without boots
and spurs. Some laugh, some hunch on their elbows,
their voices muffled under fans *whop whopping*
overhead. Some tilt their rawhide chairs,

legs crossed, their beveled boot heels cocked.
They ignore us, holding their smokes
in stained fingers fanned out.
They stare at each other, squinting
and nodding slowly.

Sleeping on Cots at Lake Buchanan

Tonight we understand the half-moon
on our pillows, raggedy moon
slanting between mesquite trees
flouncing in the wind like crones
pretending to dance Swan Lake.

This deep in Texas even the stars
are cactus, the air is green sweat,
mosquitoes, a hint of skunk.
Anything sliding under us
carries a rattle tip-up and hungry.

One far-off outboard
cruises for bass like a buzz saw.
Down at the lighted dock,
night crawlers drown,
writhing like hydras

impaled on hooks of old men
who won't give up
this close to midnight,
huddled under a yellow moon
slanted in its own strange joy.

Leaving a Boat on the Brazos

Kicking at the boat
sunk in backwater, green paint
flaking off the gunwale,
we feel the rotting wood

give way under our boots
like a dream at the edge of morning.
Water bugs skate over the boat,
pause, skate again

past minnows darting
and gliding in the bow.
Whoever rowed it here
that last time years ago

must have tired of dipping
the lake with a bait bucket,
beached it and left it
to rot like a horse in the desert.

It is the way all good dreams
have to end, with a real lake
or sunshine seeping in,
bass and bluegills

swimming away out of reach,
the dreamer stepping out
on solid ground with his bait
and tackle and going on.

COMING HOME

1.

Crustaceans hatch in stone pools
in Arizona, when it rains.
They lay their eggs and die.
We can imagine final facts,

and we've seen babies,
the orderly beginnings of others.
But time before we were
leaves us gasping like fish

stranded in sand.
Surely we have always
breathed. Can something
believe, finite as we are,

we're worth it? On a beach,
hands clawing through sand
sometimes find sudden splendors—
doubloons, Krugerrands.

A baby being born may hear
clinical whispers
after hours of labor.
Not even the host body feels the incision

in a hand that knows
about beginnings. Think of the blade
slicing an inch from eyes
that still can't see.

2.

Stones and arroyos
drop behind and we are home,
the plains level before us,

cotton like snow
puffed over cobblestones.
The sun is polished bronze,

the road, hot oil and rubber.
Our tires sing
the old story of journeys,

wind in the rigging,
family and friends
lining the shore sparkling

though it's only sand,
skiffs shoving out with garlands
from our own gardens.

OUT OF THE WHIRLWIND

GRANDFATHER'S FARM NEAR MORTON

These are fields to walk away from, weedy,
fallow for three wars. Of course it's ours,
but how far down before it's Texas?
Sand drifts up like tumbleweeds.

Grandfather leased it for oil and moved
four years before Pearl Harbor. They've
never drilled a well. Geologists and sand
don't lie. There's nothing here worth sweat.

His mules are here under drifts like graves.
This hill may be the tractor; that,
the collapsed outhouse platted on the map.
For dirt, we'd have to drain sand like a sea,

raise a fence so high against more sand
neighbors would complain. Steel plows
could break dirt hard as adobe. But only
on weekends, as a hobby, no late nights

witching for water, no digging myself to death
on stones deep as the earth's core, planting
by tractor light, trying to make flat fields
say wheat and maize as well as sand.

WITCHING

Farming on dry land, a man keeps his witch-stick
handy. It might be dark little pepper clouds
at night, maybe a coyote lame in the hip
and desperate, cramming his head
through the chicken wire and choked to death.

Something will give a sign, and faith aside,
you go witching. Women I know like willows,
most men take oak or sycamore. If Zacchaeus
could see the Lord from a sycamore,
my Uncle Murphy used to say, the same branch
ought to point me to the water of life.

But it's maple for me, the peeled crotch
bone-white and hollow in the heartwood,
tiny tubes that sough in the wind like ghosts
I hear offering advice. *Go,*
they moan so low I sometimes think I'm dreaming,
Go. And I go that way for a while, the maple
dragging the other way. I've seen my daddy
bring them in five times a summer. The record
is six, one short of perfect.

I've wondered if it isn't this land I keep
scratching to make a living, hardpan,
ten inches of rain a year, flat
as the day Columbus was born. I've seen wells
brought in elsewhere in Texas. With my own eyes.

ON THE FARM

Bury the cradled moon
and let wild geese fly over.
Even the stuttering owl
knows music. All dark

is filled with chords,
nights we listen so late
we're alone, still enough
to let all human breath slow

closer to death. Only then,
fearing all evil, rodents
run out on tiny claws
tapping a tympanum of dust

under owls and a quarter moon.
We dream in a world of fierce
harmonics, swift wings that dive
and winnow the night for song.

THE WITNESS OF DRY PLAINS

Often in my fields I see mesquite trees
    balanced on one trunk pretending to be
green flamingos. Wind in the west

does that, shaking their leaves
    like feathers. Cactus and snakes
beg it won't ever rain. I'd do it

a different way, if I made pastures.
    These dry, bone-scattered plains go on
forever, flat as a pelt on a highway

dozens of pickups pound flatter
    daily, until not even buzzards
can resurrect it—coyote or armadillo,

whatever it was in its last appetite
    crossing the road. Living on thermals,
a hawk rises high in the heavens,

blessing each shadow with feathers
    of each wing, seeing one rabbit
hop into sunlight, and diving,

wings stiff and wide, totally silent.
    All is as it will be, in a desert.
Even the trees are balanced.

LIVING ON OPEN PLAINS

Flat words for flat land,
wide as a state. Flat is a state
of mind. Imagine driving for hours

without one hill, the cruise control
asleep on sixty. Nothing but yucca,
red cactus blossoms, pale green mesquite

balanced on single trunks, pretending to be
flamingoes. Buzzards spiral on thermals
over the road. If we're lucky,

a hawk at dawn. At night, a coyote
begging the moon. We plant imported willows
and make believe they're native.

Think of a forest laid tree to tree
across a desert: the Santa Fe freight train
speeds by a quarter-mile away at noon.

Two crewmen, one in the caboose.
Our children run outside and wave
like people frantic, stranded. I think

the crewmen wave. A long sad whistle
starts, but not for us:
for that dirt crossing farther on.

Open Country

The banks are closed
against today's red sky.
Nothing not in vaults
is safe. Sandstorms
ride into town like
Sherman tanks at forty
miles an hour, commanders
grimy and goggled, elbows
wedged on the turrets,
glancing neither left
nor right, crashing through
willows, swirling dust
into the oatmeal of old men,
setting the spring town's
teeth on edge, a dry run
for tornadoes.

SANDSTORMS

How many nights can we take it,
the constant blither of wind,
the splatting of sand

on the windows? We would pray
for rain, even floods,
here where nothing comes of all

our tossing and turning, trying
to sleep, but dust in the morning
to whisk away with oilcloths.

Nothing can keep it out,
not locks, not wet towels
plastered to the cracks. Dust

floats through every slant of light
and settles. Even our feet
as we tip-toe tap up a plume,

a soft tattoo of dust that follows
everywhere, an echo of outside
weather. We wash sheets

twice a week and slip between
clean percale already grainy,
our bodies rubbing away to dust.

CROSSWINDS

Pilots know wind blows where it wills,
some days never straight down a runway,
learn to slip planes through crosswinds,
wing low, mashing opposite rudder

to keep from turning, a feeling of falling.
Even in a gale, this brings you straight,
aiming for centerline down final,
trusting the tilted earth like vertigo.

Crabbing into the wind is simpler,
approaching crosswise,
balanced between heading
and touchdown. Over the runway,

rounded out, power off and dying, you have to
kick the rudder hard to line up
at impact. Too soon, the wind
drifts you, struts buckling like a knee.

Too late, you slam down hard
like breaking an ankle. Airplanes
landing on broken struts can burn.
It is a pilot's choice, like love,

falling straight ahead, slipping
off balance, or sideways into the wind
like a hermit crab, making your move
either way at the last moment.

Commitment either way is crucial.
In a stiff wind, wing severely dipped
to keep the glide path steady,
you watch the ground loom up

and guess the angle. Too steep,
the wingtip touches, digs
and flips the airplane cartwheeling
in flames. Time it, time it

to clear the runway, cut power
and flare a few feet level,
hold off and lift the wingtip,
floating toward concrete

like a couple coming together,
wings straight against the wind
as airspeed stalls
and the wheels touch.

Out of the Whirlwind

Because the land plays out
we're needed.
Nothing in the world feeds us
but dirt. We bury
barrels of iron in sand,

plow magic into farms
dying for nitrogen. We tap
stone pipes in semi-arid zones
and water bumper crops.
After a hail, we squat

among stripped stalks
and shake drenched cotton
in our fists, shake them
at black clouds rumbling east.
Something in the skies

seems foreign, sometimes drought
or sleet, never enough rain
or sun. We believe
given the time
we could reap the moon.

Out of the whirlwinds,
meat. Out of leeched clay,
milk. If we believe
hard work brings wheat
and cattle, we are fed.

DRILLING ON DRY LAND

Witching, a man sees
how little earth there is.
Brown grass-stubble clings to caliche.

Down between mesas in canyons
where it collects, only an inch of dirt,
never enough for plows. I live out here

year after year with a witch stick,
trying to wring water from rock,
and I'm no prophet. Nothing is certain

but heat and mesquites that send thin
taproots deep enough to live
through any drought. My cattle wade

up to their knees in alkali flats
drinking the last drying playa lakes.
Mortgaging the house, I borrow from the bank

again and hire a rig, tighten the nuts
and ease the drill bit down over stone,
step back and hit the switch.

LEVELS

We watch the last train
clicking past, dragging a sound
long after the lights are gone,
no other echoes but jets

high in a black sky,
people we'll never see
rising and strolling the rows
over our farm. A stewardess

may glance out at the dark
while she waits handing vodka
to a man reaching his card
to someone by the window.

Between them, a child
crossing a continent to visit daddy
thinks of her mother
back at the airport

waving goodbye.
The pilot points at another jet's
contrails crossing above them,
but passengers sipping drinks

flip pages with lagoons
they'll never see,
or if they do glance up,
all they see are lights.

86

SOARING AT MARFA

Windows down, we drive
hundreds of flat miles
to the western edge of Texas,
heat waves shimmering

like ghosts of rattlers,
crushed armadillos
our mile-markers,
the hint of skunk.

Trees are ocotillo cactus
buzzards should be circling.
In this desert we expect
to glance up from road maps

and see lost Dutchmen
leading burros, searching
for harbors, the gold of India,
the way we hope for heat

the hotter the better
to burn away what ails us,
sailplane boxed in a trailer,
wings off, tow line stowed,

the Marfa airport
our promised land,
nothing in the sky but sun,
the strongest thermals.

Prairie Dogs Live in Lubbock

except a few hundred in colonies
near towns like Muleshoe, Midland,
and Littlefield. All others
have disappeared, starved by farmers,

poisoned, wiped out in thousands
by the plague that rides from colony
to colony like royalty
in the cushioned stomachs of fleas.

Ranchers hate varmints, losing good mounts,
forelegs snapped by their holes. Once,
boys could stand a mile out of town
and shoot at dogs with .22's all day.

Now, the city's Prairie Dog Town
has a wall and a law against molesting
the hundred rodents which scamper
like rabbits, stand on hind legs

and try to bark, and the dozen or so
owls that squat like ceramics.
Young couples bring their children
to feed prairie dogs once or twice

over the years. And sometimes
in the cool of evening, old people
driving slow will idle by the fence
and watch them bark awhile.

DUST DEVILS

Here is where heaven starts,
wind like the spirit of peace

blowing sand in our eyes
for weeks. Spring on the plains

is a month of static and storms
without clouds, the blustery days

dry as fields fallow all winter,
the sand like our own souls

naked, harrowed and seedless,
waiting to be given wings.

LIVING IN NEXT-YEAR COUNTRY

We feed hardscrabble sand
green manure from a dairy. Seeds
we sprinkle like silver iodide
dry up and blow away. Nights, after hoeing
stalks trying to survive another drought,

we collapse, sipping homemade beer
from depression glass. We add and multiply
by lamplight, as if paper calves
could turn to cows. We should give up
on schemes to make this prairie dust

grow hooves. My father said Texas is
next-year country—next year it may rain,
next year we'll make two cotton bales to an acre
and buy a bull. We'd rather starve
than move away from land so flat it's ours.

The only asphalt road goes straight
a mile away. Even our dogs are farmers.
They drag home bones they find on other farms,
gnaw them dry and plant them. Unless it rains,
we'll never raise alfalfa for one calf.

Cow bones buried in the field may grow a herd
before we can. We sit outside at noon
under our only oak and watch hawks stalking snakes.
Wheeling, rising on thermals, they search for hours,
gliding in a sky so blank they stare.

THE FARM AT AUCTION

It's gone, let garbled voices
auctioneer no more. The one bold gavel
gags us: *sold.* Don't give them tears,

it's over. Strange men in denim,
dealers, bidders from out of county
feel of my plows and heifers

like men reaching under my own wife's
dress, neighbors looking on,
my children standing by themselves

and staring. One grown farmer
could raise all the cotton
dirt could grow, if the bank

would let him, if foreign markets
stayed the same, if diesel didn't turn
to gold. Something in the sky

turned its back on us overnight,
something we've cursed but worked with
all these years—the threat of hail,

too little rain before harvest,
the reasonable gamble of sweat
in all seasons. How many times

do they sell all you own
to high bidders? Eighty dollars
to take that ditcher off my hands,

thank you for nothing. I paid
a thousand new and the paint's
not scratched, the blade is silver

from clay I broke it through.
I should be used to this by now,
plowing flat fields for nothing

I can keep. Come on, lift up your end
of this oak hope chest and heave it
aboard. There's room in the pickup

for this and more, but not for tears.
Lift up your city head
and look around: it's gone.

WITHOUT FEAR OF FLYING

CROP DUSTING IN A BIPLANE

Crop dusting on hardscrabble,
a man keeps his wind sock working.
It might be tight little pepper clouds
overhead, or dustdevils on the horizon,
but if you trust only your luck

fickle wind can kill you.
Even on a strip dragged flat
by a rented grader, two headings,
east and west, you check prevailing
gusts while cranking up,

grounding magnetos, watching the rpm fall
like a barometer, the propeller shaking
both thin wings of your Waco.
When the wind sock flips six times
in one direction, you taxi out

and trust it as you do your gauges,
more to worry about than wind—how many
telephone wires at the next farm,
how many flights until harvest, how many G's
a wing strut pulls before breaking.

Looking out on the Morning

I open the curtains,
the fine dust spinning
like galaxies.

How many nights lying
together in darkness and nothing
stopping, nothing at all—

our children spinning off
on their own, their cars
breaking down, their health

precarious as a telephone
about to ring, even the dogs
swelling with tumors,

chain links tightening
daily around the world, the good
photographs of our wedding

beginning to peel,
brittle as pottery
composed of too much sand.

We scold our last son,
cajole, pray under cover
of night for light to come,

our son to grow up
gentle with others, gentle
with himself, his good right hand

closing and opening curtains
on a world of dust
and light worth seeing.

LEARNING THE STORY OF SCARS

After the axe-head buried itself
in his ankle, my father clung to the log
he was splitting, squeezing his eyes
like fists. Twelve, he logged those woods
for years with his father—Arkansas,
the great depression, doing whatever they could.

Groaning, he jerked and jerked the axe
like a pump handle, he screamed
and went on pumping until the foot fell back,
hinged by the ankle, white and spurting.
With a bandana he held it and held it
while Arkansas flooded, and saw his father
running, his own axe raised ready to kill
whatever snake slashed the heel of his son.

I learned that scar like a tree
split by lightning, healed over,
knew my father had in him a boy
who had suffered alone in a forest.

Going Away Together

Parked under a shelter
between Laredo and Zapata,
we watch heat shimmer on Lake Falcon.

This rest stop is a table
and trash barrel,
a scattering of cactus

curled like boxers' ears,
board steps going over
a barbed-wire fence.

Out on Falcon
wind whips white caps
like the sea.

One cabin boat
plunges like a freighter,
all hands below deck.

We've come to test the reservoir's
legends of deep water,
lake trout the size of sharks.

Back in the car
we clatter over flint rocks
toward Zapata

and the night's cabin,
glancing at waves crashing,
the one boat disappeared.

We have faith
in the buoyancy of boats
and marriage, but pray

for calm tomorrow,
for summer days
hotter than desire.

Our tires sing for the winds
to die, for trout to rise
to whatever bait we cast.

Each in Its Element

Long after dark,
twigs snap. Prowlers,
or bass leaping
along the dock.

We could believe the sky
falls into space,
the stratosphere is
pierced and leaking,

if we listened
to our breath too long
at night. Breathe,
and breathe in nothing

we can touch.
We live like bass
leaping into air
where moths hover,

but holding their breath
until deep in the water,
seeing nothing
but water, believing

as long as gills keep
blinking like eyelids,
as long as there is water,
there is air.

Double Mountain Fork of the Brazos

Living on stones and runoff from rain
that rarely comes, this fork in forty miles
drains dust, dry mouth swearing
all it owns to the Brazos.

Whoever named it liked romance,
mountains two hundred miles away,
nothing where it begins
but a sudden drop-off in a field,

a sinkhole twenty feet across.
I've stood there, seen
a mighty river start, if I believed
in names. I've backpacked forty miles

and never found a stream so deep
I couldn't step across on stones.
I slept under train trestles so low
I almost bumped my head.

I named creatures living on nothing
but each other, coyotes and skunks,
owls, a thousand diamondbacks, rabbits
with wide eyes and rapidly beating hearts.

HOME

Not when the wind
kicks up in the west
and turns the sky

blood-red, but later,
when fallout
powders all dark wood

is when the plains soul
feels at home.
Dust, and dust for hours

and watch it swirl
in a slant of light
and settle.

ON A SCREENED PORCH IN THE COUNTRY

I'm sleeping off August
on the porch swing,
you're propped against a post,

sketching. Dulled
by work and cicadas,
I feel your charcoal

slice me better than I am,
a deft excision here,
a tuck to tighten skin

below the eyes. I rise
creaking like old canvas
to bring you whatever

you still see, after I stretch
and hobble on a bone spur
and stiff knees to the rail.

AUGUST ON PADRE ISLAND

This is no season for old men,
yet here we sit
under beach umbrellas
as if shade could save us.

This sun strips the breath
down to the bone.
Gull feathers fall,
white sails in the Gulf

die for a breeze. Splashing
as waves crash over them,
children puff like balloons
and dive. Cool currents

slide over them like eels.
They burst straight up,
squealing, leaping in a season
that never lasts.

Mainly the Values Change

So much is overrated,
the morning news, rubies
and other stones,
sex before forty.

What matters most is who,
not what or when,
and why, not where—
strolling the beach

better than
jack-knife dives
when we were twenty,
your brittle teeth

worth more
than all trophies.

The Waves at Padre Island

Riding the waves at Padre Island,
we paddle black innertubes
that lift and drop sharply in each trough.

How many times our children rose
and fell on these balloons
which never sink, which don't leak even now

for two grandparents wallowing
like kids. Those years, we waded
bobbing in the Gulf to save

spilled babies from the undertow.
Later, we watched them from the beach,
big children swimming farther out

than we dared, these innertubes
like stranded jellyfish. Now, leaned back
on round tight rubber, we swirl

like children on a tilt-a-whirl, spinning
the rest of our lives, laughing
with no one to hear, gasping when one wave

suddenly drops, our eyes
hardly squinting, able to bear
the blunt sea-level sun.

At Port Aransas

Cars towing boats move ten car-lengths
an hour, a single ferry, the scenic way
to the mainland. We could backtrack
to the bridge, but we have come so far.

Girls bronzed and bikinied pose
head-back by sports cars. Muscles
from nowhere start flicking frisbees.
The sun rises above the Gulf.

The line moves up. Muscles carry Corvettes
like barbells. They lean on the girls'
hoods, and girls cling to their biceps.
At noon, we buy fish and chips

from a vendor, eat greasy food in our
oven of a car. Gulls glide and sidle
in the breeze like albino buzzards
stalking a caravan. All day we nag

and forgive each other, take turns
napping and reading the same flat map
that led us here. Sun going down,
we hear the ferry's foghorn, and realize

we're next. We listen to waves rush
and recede, and strain to find boats
falling off the horizon, even the great ships
sinking toward open ocean.

Alone in a Windstorm

These are the fallen apples,
the proof of wind, the roots' labors.
All night in the storm
we lay touching, alone at last,

our children scattered
this autumn weekend.
The dogs stumble
as our rakes go back, go back

under the cracked branches.
We rake up apples like winnings
and count our losses by the bushel.
We touch the hail-stripped limbs

and sever all we must.
After rain and raking, the grass
is greener than we've ever noticed.
All afternoon we're sleepy,

fatigue that saves us
for another night, no matter
how hard the hot wind blows
or if the whole crop falls.

FISHING AT FORT HOOD

Another bass breaks the water
thrashing, falls back
and leaps again, the hook
reeling him in under the stars.

A boom like thunder.
One light on the lake
would be too much,
a man and his father able to gauge

the catch by feel. We give back
to water all but the best,
our first night together in months,
the Army's way of making the heart

grow fonder, two men alone
on a government lake in Texas,
my son's fringe benefits
for serving time in khaki—

boat signed out in his name,
rods and reels, a bank
perfect for plugging, bass
rising out of a dredged lake

attacking whatever bait we toss,
fighting like soldiers
for every inch of their lives,
the best bass-fishing ever.

He tells me which sector
tanks rumble down tonight in bivouac,
mock battles building like a front,
cannons booming, bass striking every cast

like in a rainstorm, mosquitoes
drawing blood all night.
Caught on a hook deep down,
we slap and go on reeling.

Without Fear of Flying

When we are young we'll fly
anything with wings, step out in space
and fall for miles, believing silk canopies
safe as the buffer of years.

Living to middle age extends metaphor
past first layovers, patient for connections,
accepting any in-flight movie they serve,
knowing warning lights may flash,
no seat belts hold us safe
in case of metal fatigue or bombs.

I imagine growing old is more
than letting down through clouds at night
in Minnesota, suddenly breaking out
near a terminal alone on snowfields
stretching past frozen lakes to Canada,
to ice caps we already feel, as the engines whine
and we grip the armrests, lean back
and the wheels touch.

ICE FISHING

Moving our hooks to keep from freezing,
we camped on a lake so white the crows
seemed blinded, crouched in the tree tops,
cawing for alms. We picked the spot the way

we choose our lives, triangulating
among desires and luck, remembering pines,
these pines. We believed trout hovered
ten meters down, dreaming of runoff,

our hooks the bait they'd wake to.
Each day we promised we'd bring back
trout too thick for skillets.
Each day we claimed the ice again,

sawing until our slick skin glazed.
At dusk we ate our loaves and fish
and watched our rented smoke across the lake
curl up and disappear. We remembered

our wives in summer, turning to gold
in water. Planes flew over low and circled
as if they'd never seen a lake before
with people fishing for their lives.

When they flew on, nothing made a sound
but begging crows, and suddenly a trout,
reeled in and slapping on the ice.
We said a few more of those would last

a lifetime, and buried our hooks
past midnight, our springing rod tips
pointing to the north star,
nothing in our creels but fish.

How the Records Fell

This time there seemed no stopping it,
fog for days, mist turning to rain,
to freezing rain, to crystal trees,

clear ice that cracked
and crushed all cars parked under.
We watched snow fill the streets by noon.

By dusk, huddled with coffee mugs,
we saw snow flood the dark so deep
the shrubs went under. All night

we raised up from time to time
and stared and lay back down
and held each other.

WONDERS OF THE WORLD

Our son leaves early with his wife
and daughter. Outside this condo
north of Dillon, we wave them away
in jackets and dark glasses, stunned

to see them curve so suddenly
beyond the pines. After they've gone,
we salvage what we can, searching the slopes
for signs—our son's bold swathes,

footprints, the mitten Jennifer lost.
Snow falls for hours, five new inches
of powder. We putter inside, packing,
picking at leftovers, sorting scraps

for jays before we leave for home. We build
one final fire and share the Polaroids,
already aging, like the museum in Denver
where they've gone to show a child

more frozen wonders of the world—
stuffed bears, stacked bones
of dinosaurs towering above her,
the locked display of Colorado gold.

In the Attic

Here under the roof, humped over,
we steal short breaths like
snorkeling, to keep from snorting dust
like plankton floating in the attic.

What we need lies buried in a trunk
under layers of silt—baby clothes
wrapped in tissues, old photo albums,
copper bracelets like doubloons.

They're grown, with babies of their own,
home for the holidays. We asked
if they remember that fishing trip
with their Great Uncle Joe,

the hugs of Great-Grandmother Hunt,
the medals of Great-Grandfather who fought
in Flanders, and they smiled like neighbors
and said no. It's all up there,

we promised, and crawled up. Now,
kneeled in the dust of voices
even we have to strain to remember,
we lift the lid, sift through old clothes

and bedspreads we wonder why we've saved.
Lifting out keepsakes, the brittle
gallery albums like parchments,
we climb down into natural light

of the garage, snug shut the plywood
overhead and brush each other. We enter
the living room with our family together
the only time in years, drapes wide,

the light almost too much for our eyes,
and reveal amazing faces of ancestors
to our children, the stiff black and whites
of people younger than themselves.

JACOB'S CEILING

These are the nickel nights,
the buffalo coins
of childhood. Here, lying flat
on the floor and kicking,
our grandson's wide eyes
sees magic in the flecked,
textured plaster of the ceiling
like millions of beasts
grazing flat plains. Jacob
in snap-pajamas tries
flying to them,
reach-kick-kick, huffing
at six months, at home
under ceiling lights and fan blades
turning his eyes around
and around like a mobile.
His voice chuffs a nonsense
music. His fists
no bigger than my finger
rise before him like a conductor's
using no baton. His feet
kick-thrust a rhythm
all his own.
The fan keeps whirling,
and buffalo herds
or angels we've forgotten
wheel in ceiling-fan shadows around
and around in carrousels
Jacob believes.

SETTING OUT OAKS IN WINTER

No trees stay green all summer here,
heat-stressed, blighted,
full of drought. Nothing thrives
by itself without climate
I can't promise—wind gusts within reason,

rain more than twice a year,
enough birds to eat the leaf lice. The wind
is foreign, and even with silver iodide
and prayer, it rains only when it rains.
Birds fly over every year, a desert

between snow and tropics. We breed our own
with baths and feeders in the yard
high off the ground above the dogs.
In winter, since dry land never freezes,
we dig through sand to white caliche

and throw in loam like pennies, lift
bought trees balled up in burlap
and swing them overboard like treasure.
The only way these trees survive
is like love, anchored to posts

in the ground like blessings
against the winds, pruning
what isn't required, soaking them
over and over with water
pumped from our own deep wells.